'Ta-ra-a-Bi

CW00351349

A little book of language used by 'Brummies'

By Stephen Burrows & Michael Layton

First Published by Bostin Books February 2018.
Second, expanded edition March 2020

This little book is dedicated to all 'Brummies'
wherever they are. I hope is that it brings back fond
memories, and a smile to the fizzogs of readers.

Other books by Michael Layton and Stephen Burrows

Joint:
Historical Fiction:
Black Over Bill's Mother's – A Storm is Coming
Keep Right On
The Touch Of Innocence
Non-Fiction:
One in For D & D – a little book of police slang
It's A Blag – police tricks and funny stories
Reporting for Duty – West Midlands Police (The first twenty-five years 1974 – 1999)
Top Secret Worcestershire
The Noble Cause
Walsall's Front Line – Volume 1 (1997-1998)
Walsall's Front Line – Volume 2 (1998-1999)

By Michael Layton

Non-Fiction:
Hunting the Hooligans (With Robert Endeacott)
Tracking the Hooligans (With Alan Pacey)
Police Dog Heroes (With Bill Rogerson)
Birmingham's Front Line
Violence in the Sun
The Night the Owl Cried - A Taste of Cyprus (With Androulla Christou-Layton)
The Hooligans Are Still Among Us (With Bill Rogerson)
By Stephen Burrows

Historical Fiction
Pretty Thing

Introduction

I was inspired to compile this 'bostin' little book by a Facebook post that went 'viral'. The post contained a few Brummie expressions that my co-author, Mike Layton and I, had compiled for authenticity purposes to use in our Birmingham focused novels.

The interest shown was overwhelming. The phrases came from our memories of growing up in the City, with many of them used by us, as well as our parents and grandparents. Just writing down these few words and phrases brought back both memories and laughter.

Mike and I are *'baby boomer'* Brummies, and descendants of several generations of Brummies. Mike lived in Wheeler Street, Lozells, whilst I lived in Moseley for my first twenty-five years. We both still retain the accent and use terms such as *'traffic island'* and *'gambol'* without fully realising their local nature and history – that is until now.

The original post was shared on social media many times and attracted literally hundreds of comments. There was much humour, especially as a number of offspring, friends and family, realised that these funny phrases used by their parents and partners were actually genuine!

Many people asked for a translation and whether a collation of terms could be produced. Here it is!

***

A Word On Origins

This book has been written for fun.

I am not a student of etymology (historical language change), and make no claims of expertise, I have just done my best.

Some of the contents of this book are of Brummie origin, many are from the Black Country, whilst some are involved in an endless tug of war for ownership. Others may come from the Midlands or further afield. This book is **not claiming Birmingham ownership for any of them, just usage.**

In particular, the geographical proximity of Birmingham to the Black Country leaves little doubt that many slang terms originated in the Black Country and have subsequently been given a Brummie pronunciation.

It would take many years of research and expertise in the history of language to definitively trace and locate the origins of the words and phrases – if that were indeed possible.

English /Anglo-Saxon is itself a conglomeration of words from all over the world, especially Scandinavia and Europe, and further back, Latin, so solving the question of ultimate ownership is a fairly pointless and fruitless endeavor.

If you add the fact that the population of the United Kingdom has, since the Industrial Revolution, been highly migratory, particularly from rural villages to the new big cities such as Birmingham, it is not surprising that local language gets moved with the people.

The advent of the internet has added a more significant and all – pervasive means of both spreading and 'standardising' language, so younger readers may think that some phrases now in common usage were not once very local in their genesis – they were. The internet also means that those with memories only going back twenty years or so may think that phrases are 'theirs', when they have simply become universal.

The internet is killing local dialect and sayings and replacing them with (mainly) American English and text speak, so it is ever more important to preserve our rich heritage of language. This book is a (hopefully) humorous attempt to do so.

So all this book is claiming, is that these words and phrases were/are in use in Birmingham, and some have been so for a very long time – wherever they originally came from.

In the end, does it matter? The really important thing is to treasure, preserve, laugh at, and use them. Language is part of our heritage and belongs to us.

***

A Note On Pronunciation

A joke for Brummies:

'What is the difference between a Buffalo and a Bison?' You can only wash your hands in a *'Bison'*.

The Brummie accent is much abused, rarely correctly imitated, full of warmth and humour, and almost impossible to recreate on the page.

Without being spoken, some of the following words and phrases lose their individual Brummie character. I have tried, where possible to indicate pronunciation, but my recommendation is to seek out your oldest living Brummie relative and get them to say them.

As a general rule though, forget any 'H's at the start of words, and 'G's at the end – unless it's *'Garding'* (Garden), which has the benefit of a bonus 'G' in Birmingham.

I have made a valiant attempt to group the contents as sayings, action words and descriptive words to keep it in some sort of order, some are all three, but it doesn't really matter. It is not a dictionary!

Have fun, *'ere we go!'*

(Stephen Burrows 2018)

Figure 1 Me Dad with other engineers at the Land Rover in the 1950's

PART ONE

SAYINGS

Never in the rain/ reign of Pig's Pudding

Let's start with a good one. It means that it will never happen, whatever it is. It was very widely used in Birmingham in the past. I cannot find any information on its origins. Pig's Pudding is Black Pudding but why and whether it rains or reigns is a good question. Either way, it's not going to happen.

*

A face like fourpence / a smacked arse / A face as long as Livery Street

Someone is looking miserable. There are other local dialect phrases concerning four- pence and they all seem to revolve around an item that was too expensive at four- pence and would be left on the shelf. Perhaps that made it look miserable, and what child with a smacked arse looks happy? Livery Street still exists and is a very long road – oroight?

And whilst we are on the subject of faces....

—

9

*

A face like a bosted boot / arse / welder's bench / bag of spanners /back of a bus/ rough as a goat's knee/rough as a bear's arse

I'm afraid that you are not a pretty sight, or worse for wear. Both the rural and industrial influences are clear. (The bear? Well, the Warwickshire emblem is the Bear and Ragged Staff...) Useful descriptions – preferably out of earshot of the subject!

*

Ark at that rain / Ark at er

In true Brummie tradition the 'H' has gone AWOL, (Absent Without Official Leave), but this is clearly a derivative of the old word 'Hark' as in 'Hark The Herald Angels', but there were clearly other things to listen to in Birmingham, like 'er next door gooin on'. Hark derives from the Middle English word 'herk' meaning to listen or hear by the way.

*

Use a Birmingham Screwdriver

Dad was an engineer and used this phrase all the time.
If something gets stuck, hit it with a big hammer.
Never fails.....to break something.

*

(Going) All Around The Wrekin

Beating about the bush, not getting to the point. The
Wrekin is a big hill in Shropshire and I suspect that
the Brums went on day trips out there, before package
holidays to Torremolinos became affordable.

*

(It's a bit) Black over Bill's Mother's

It's gonna piss down in a bit Bab. Nottinghamshire
folk are adamant that this relates to some farmer up
that way, but this saying has been used in
Birmingham for generations.

Both Professor Carl Chinn and the BBC have
concluded that the most likely explanation is that
'Bill's Mother' is Mary Arden, 'Bill' Shakespeare's
Mom, and the location is her house in Stratford,
which is of course preserved and has been a day trip
destination for generations of Brummies. The

prevailing weather is supposed to come from that direction, bringing storms. That is good enough for me, our kid.

The saying may go back even further, having been brought to Birmingham by Warwickshire agricultural workers moving to the city during the Industrial Revolution.

This is also the title of a Bostin book by Steve Burrows and Michael Layton. (Got to gerra plug in ain't ya?)

*

(Your mom / sister works at) The back of Rackhams

Your female relative is a lady of the night. This phrase is One Hundred Per Cent Brummie. It is incredible that generations of Brummies know what this means, when any evidence of this place being a red light area is extremely old (1700's), and vague.

*

Any road up

Anyway, to get to the point of, or return to the

original subject of the conversation.... Also, this was the title of Birmingham group, The Steve Gibbon's Band's, first LP, released in 1976 – which shows it was a well-known saying in Birmingham back then.

*

Gerrin on me wick

You are annoying me. This is in fact from Cockney Rhyming slang. Wick is from Hampton Wick, slang for 'prick'. The slang seems to have originated from use by soldiers in World War II.

*

Got a right cob on

Annoyed or sulking. Widespread nationally and probably not Brummie in origin, but used in the city.

*

(You look like) A sack of spuds / bag of rags tied round the middle

Your dress sense leaves something to be desired...Probably has agricultural origins, coupled

---

with memories of the urban life of the poor.

*

For the umpteenth time

How many times have I got to tell you? The word 'umpteenth' has an interesting history. An 'umpty' was a slang term originally referring to a Morse Code dash but became the word for an indefinitely large number. The 'teenth' bit just makes it sound better, like 'nineteenth'.

*

Red hat, no drawers / Fur coat no knickers / all kippers and curtains

Dresses or acts posh, but really hasn't a 'hapeth' to rub together. Local consensus was that prostitutes wore red hats, hence the lack of knickers.

*

Ee knows ow many beans make five

He knows stuff, or is clever. One can reasonably assume that this dates back to the agricultural forefathers of Brummies. There was apparently a correct answer, 'a bean and a half, a bean and a half, half a bean and a bean and a half.' How that makes one clever remains thankfully lost in time.

*

Gerrout of it!

Don't be daft, or I don't believe you.

*

Never in a month of Sundays

It's not happening, it will take forever or I'm not doing it. Dates back to at least the Eighteenth Century. Traditionally Sundays were long' boring days where nothing was open and activity was limited. A month of Sundays takes about thirty weeks – seeming like forever.

*

Got a bob on isself

Someone with 'airs and graces', an ego. Mom used to call them 'affected' but I've never heard anyone else use that phrase.

*

Borrow us a ..

A classic Brummie phrase meaning, lend me something. Why not use 'lend? Who knows or cares, it's just great.

*

I'll go to the foot of our stairs

I am amazed and surprised. Northern in origin, but adopted by Brummies generations ago. Probably something to do with having a walk to recover equanimity – or even 'I'm off to bed I'm so surprised'.

*

(We had a) Couple or three

More than two, probably more than three, but not lots. Originates in the USA, how it got to Birmingham is anyone's guess.

*

On the Treacle Stick

On the dole. Dates back a very long way to the days of the Poor Law when Parishes gave 'relief' to the poor – or stuck them in the Workhouse. And once you were on the 'treacle stick' – you stuck.

*

Up and down like a mad woman's knickers/ breakfast / ooers drawers / yo yo / bride's nightie

Just a sample of a very generic and global phrase in English speaking countries, especially Australia. Lots of the alternatives must have specific historical origins. A useful clutch of variations to imbue your conversation with character and get you roundly condemned for being 'un PC' - your choice. Try one on Twitter and see what happens. You'll get a response.

*

Fair to middlin

Feel like I've got an illness coming on. 'Middling' is an old noun that denotes forthcoming illness.

*

Couldn't stop a pig in an entry

Bandy–legged. A Black Country saying used in Birmingham that is just too good to leave out - Nuff said.

*

She's bin babbied

The lady is with child.

*

Five and Twenty Past / To

How old Brummies tell the time. Forget digital displays, this dates back to proper clocks with hands.

*

There and back to see how far it is

The Brummie rejoinder to 'where ya goin?' or, 'where's ya bin?'

*

Put the wood in the hole, were you born in a barn?

Shut the bloody door before the heat gets out and costs us more money Usually uttered by long-suffering Dads who had to pay the bills. These days they lock the central heating control and insist everybody wears several jumpers (ganseys) before they'll turn it on in September.

*

They'd skin a fart for a ha'penny

Deep pockets, short arms.

*

Up the wooden hill to Bedfordshire – Down sheet Lane – and along Blanket Alley

Get to bed. I only knew the first part, but my Brummie wife remembered the lot

*

Ee's a right Peaky Blinder / Ee's a little blinder

He's smartly dressed or he's a little monster. From the 1920's, and we all know about the Peaky Blinders now. If you want to know more, look out for Professor Carl Chinn's book, *'The Real Peaky*

Blinders'.

*

What's a marrer? – A cucumbers uncle

Only the genuine Brummie accent can achieve the
pronunciation required to make this 'in joke' work.

*

I don't give a jot nor tickle

Reported as used by older Brummies. Origin obscure,
but the word 'jot' derives from 'iota' the smallest
letter in the Greek alphabet or Hebrew 'Yod' both of
which have come to represent nothing. 'Tickle' is
likely to refer to being tickled or amused by
something – or in this case not.

*

A cat lick and a promise

A cat lick is a perfunctory wash, but the phrase 'a lick
and a promise' is very old, dating back at least to the
first half of the 1800's, and means something not
done properly.

*

Go play up yer own end!

A gentle encouragement for annoying kids playing in the horse road to go and be a nuisance outside their own houses. *'Our end'* is the family homestead of a Brummie

*

You'll ave it dark

Gerra move on, its night time in a few hours.

*

This ain't gonna get the babby a new frock/ pinny/bonnet

What we are doing isn't achieving anything in money terms. We are wasting our time when we could be getting on with something productive. Black Country origin but I remember Dad using it.

*

It's like New Street Station ere

It's packed innit?

*

Avin the bags on, or Got the bags on

Annoyed about something. I can remember my Gran
saying this. 'Bags' apparently relates to boxing gloves
although there is a more modern phrase 'having the
rags on' which likely relates to menstruation and
keeping the wife away from the knife drawer.

*

I'll give you what for

I'm going to punish or scold you. Seems to stem from
the usual response to a threat of punishment - 'What
for?' Popular from the late 1800's to 1950's. Origin
obscure and is widely used in Britain. Also '*You'll
catch it*' (when yer Dad gets ome)

*

Eeyar

I am giving this to you. As opposed to Eeyore who
was the miserable donkey in 'Winnie The Pooh'.

*

I'm on the rattler

I'm on the train. Use when answering your mobile phone in the quiet carriage, at least it might bring a smile to the wearied listeners.

*

Deff it / Deaf it

Forget it. I have heard this expression used in Birmingham for fifty years but still don't know how it is spelt or where it comes from.

*

Ten arf

It is very – as in 'ten arf cold ain't it'?

*

I'll ave arf

A half of your finest ale please barman. The best Brummie girls would opt for this if you offered to buy them a drink on first meeting. No expensive Prosecco

---

and flavoured gins then.

*

Give this an eyepiece

Take a look at this

*

Got is arse in is ands

Someone who is angry. Seems to be a local phrase
but there are many variations on the word 'arse' being
used in sayings including for denoting anger, for
example 'arsey'.

*

A right bell oilin

A good beating. Black Country.

*

Cowin

An emphasizing word, substituting for a swear word.
As in Jasper Carrot's famous one liner 'Carrot they
ain't got no Cowin Bovril' in the 'Blues at Old

Trafford sketch'. Origin obscure but there is some suggestion that 'cowing' means farting in public, as cows are famously flatulent.

*

I'm on a line (with er/you)

I'm angry, exasperated or fed up with someone. This seems to be a genuine Brummie term and I can find no information on its origin elsewhere. Me Nan said it all the time, usually at me.

*

A bugger up the back / Little bugger

A little devil or nuisance. The origins of the phrases are thankfully lost in the mists of time and perhaps they should remain so.

*

Can't be arsed

Can't be bothered. Widespread in the UK, and murky in origin. Can't be arsed to investigate further.

*

Daft Apath

You stupid person, but actually has a certain fondness about it in Birmingham, so tends to be applied to a loved one. Originally Northern, and the 'apeth' is a shortening of 'halfpenny'.

*

The big Brummie mealtime problem

This can cause mayhem. A Brummie 'Dinnertime' happens in the middle of the day. 'Teatime' is the evening meal. No older Brummie will have any truck with 'lunch', 'supper' or going out for 'dinner' in the evening.

*

A voice like a glede /glead under a door

A glede is an ember, of wood or coal, spat out by a fire. The saying alludes to the screeching sound of one of these scraping on a solid floor when trapped under a door. Black Country origin.

*

Ee's in his oiltot

He is happy or satisfied. This dates back to when working men would line their stomachs with a shot of olive oil before drinking, believing it would stop them getting too drunk.

*

Up Town

Going to Birmingham City Centre. Brummies tend to go 'up' everywhere, no-one knows why. The use of 'Town' for the City Centre probably dates from before Birmingham became a City in 1889.

*

S'toim

If pronounced correctly, the average Brummie will consult their watch and let you know.

*

Titty Babby

A needy, childlike adult. Probably Southern in origin as 'titty baby', but stamped with Brummie authenticity by the change to 'babby'. Actually, 'Babby comes from the Anglo Saxon word 'babben' for baby.

*

Bab

The archetypal Brummmie term of endearment, usually, but not exclusively said by men to women and children. See above for 'Babby'.

*

Where's ya bin

No, it's not about dustbins, it means 'where have you been?' Often answered with, '*There and back to see ow far it is'*.

*

Ta

Thank you very much. A child form, dating from the 18th Century.

*

'Oright', Ow ya doin & 'Tara a bit'

Hello and Adieu, Brummie style, probably the best-known Birmingham saying, it only works with a true Brummie accent that can achieve an octave spread in pitch during vocalising.

*

Codge Up

A poorly done job. Black Country.

*

Not backwards in coming forward

Not shy and retiring

*

That's aysam – jaysam.

It's 'fair and square' is the old meaning, but I seem to remember it meaning 'all over the place'

*

Yer a daft article

Usually said with fondness rather than as an insult.

*

Like a job in the town

A really good and professional job done.

*

E's come a right purler

Falling over. From mid 19th century dialect 'purl' –
to upset or overturn.

*

Plaiting your legs

This dates back to the agricultural past when it was
observed that oxen walking appeared to plait their
legs. It later became an allusion to drunkenness but in
more modern times it has meant that you need to
urinate badly.

*

Stop playing yer face

Bit complex this one. The origin seems to relate to

———

acting – ie using one's face to portray false (acted) emotions. In Brummie it tends to be said to kids who are making a fuss about nothing.

*

I'm gonna ave a dekko at this

Means to have a look. Comes from the Hindi word 'dekho', meaning 'look'. Probably brought back from India in the 1800's

*

What's the good of a well without a bucket?

Said when someone else begins a sentence with 'well'

*

Like a fart in a colander

A description of a useless person, or one that flits about from thing to thing or place to place.

*

E'ees gonna cop out for that

He will get punished for wrongdoing.

*

Ee got a right good wiggin

Someone got a good telling off.

*

It's / he's like a dog's hind leg.

My Dad, an engineer used this to refer to something that should be straight, but wasn't. Also used for a person who is 'bent' as in 'crooked'.

*

Ee was like a dog with two dicks

In Brum this meant someone was as happy as could be.

*

That's about (h)is barrer / barrow

That just about sums him up. Or it's something that suits him – is *'right up (h)is street'*

*

(H)er's the cat's mother

Usually said by Mom when the kids are disrespectful and refer to their mother as '(H)er'

*

Figure 2 Me Mom with other Cadbury's factory guides at Bournville, circa 1950s

PART TWO

ACTIONS

To lamp

Thumping someone. Claimed by the Black Country but actually ancient in origin, possibly deriving from the Norse word 'lemja', to 'lame by beating'.

*

To thrape

The old meaning was to hit or beat someone. In more modern times, in Brum – the 'motor city', it means to thrash an engine to its extremes.

*

To Wag it

Playing truant. Another ancient phrase which is derived from 'hopping the wagon' in the UK, and later adopted by Australia. The Truant Officer is the *Waggy - man*

*

To Chobble

To crunch a hard sweet noisily. Generations of Brummie kids have been told, 'stop yer chobblin'.

*

To Scrage

To graze ones skin, usually applied to Brummie kids and their knees.

*

To Mither

To worry, moan, complain. Very old Northern English dialect, but used widely in Birmingham for generations.

*

To Blart

To cry. May derive from a sheep's 'bleat'.

*

To Gambol

To perform a forward roll. Everyone in Birmingham knows what this is, but few realise that hardly anyone else in Britain does.

*

To Goss

To spit. Seems to be Old English dialect but I had a biker mate in Brum the 70's whose nickname was 'Goss'. He has a special place in my memory because he was the first to play me the LP 'Bat Out Of Hell'.

*

To Leg It

To run away as fast as possible. There are many and varied origins of this generic phrase due to the various meanings of the word 'leg'. For example: a leg of a journey, a leg of a sailing race, the human leg. A more local explanation is the 'walking' of barges through tunnels, although it is difficult to see how this transforms into an evocation of swift movement.

*

To mooch

This has several meanings. To sponge off others, investigate; poke about a bit, skulk around. To pretend poverty or act the miser. There are two possible origins. One an ancient Old English word, 'mitch', the other French, 'muchier' – to hide or skulk.

*

To cock a deaf un

Pretend not to hear. Origin obscure.

*

To Doss around

To mess about aimlessly. Different from 'dossing' in respect of sleeping rough which is its more usual usage. Its origin as used in Birmingham seems to be unknown. Also used in this way for the phrase *'a right Doss'*, meaning something that is either really easy or requires no effort, e.g. 'This job is a right doss'. *Dosser* is a lazy person or someone sleeping rough.

*

To Slummock

To move around in an untidy or slovenly fashion.
Origin unknown, but at least mid 19th century.

*

To pither / pithering about

To mess about, prevaricate. This seems to be only
known in the Midlands and has no obvious other
origin. There is a Staffordshire dialect word 'pother',
which has a similar meaning.

*

To Bomb it

To run or drive very fast. Origin of this usage
unknown.

*

To Crash

To share – usually sweets or cigarettes as in 'crash the
ash / rocks'.

*

To Boff

To emit a noxious fart. Origin not traced.

*

To be flummoxed

Confused or puzzled. Possibly from Middle English 'flummock'. Note – used by J R R Tolkein (a Brummie), in 'The Hobbit', but much older than that.

*

To Podge (In)

To push into a queue. Seems to be a Birmingham usage. The word podge is an old English one for 'fat'.

*

To Trap / Trapping

To walk, to get walking fast, leave – 'let's trap'. 'Must trap'.

*

To dout

No, it's not spelt wrong. This is another type of doubt. To put something out, usually used as in 'dout me fag'. Possibly derived from Middle English 'don ut', (do out).

*

To Grizzle

To complain or snivel.

*

To be Chuffed

To be happy. A very old word deriving from 'Chuff' which hundreds of years ago meant swollen with fat. At this time only the rich could be fat so being fat became synonymous with being content.

*

To Ag.

To nag or pester. 'Stop yer agging'

*

To Bagsy

To claim or reserve something

*

To clock

Nothing to do with time. It means to notice someone or something.

*

To cotton on / onto

Now it means to gain an understanding of something. It dates back hundreds of years and originally meant to form an attachment or friendship. One explanation is that wet cotton is very clingy.

*

To create

To make a fuss about something.

*

To stick in your craw

Can't accept something. Literally something that is 'hard to swallow'. A craw is part of the digestive system of a bird. They swallow pebbles to help break up and digest food. If they swallow one too large and it sticks in their craw they die of starvation.

*

To Faddle

This means to bother – as in *'Can't be faddled'*.

*

Figure 3 Me Brummie Nan in er pinny

PART THREE

DESCRIPTIVE WORDS

Miskin (men)

The dustbin / dustbin men. Derives from an old
Midlands word 'mixen', which means dungheap or
'midden'.

*

The Buzz

The local **Wumpty,** (West Midlands Passenger
Transport Executive) omnibus, the best known of
which is the Number 11, 'Outer Circle'.

*

Gassin

Gossiping, chatting, usually used when there are other
things to do.

*

Suff

A drain. Claimed by both the Black Country and Staffordshire. Common usage in the past in Birmingham.

*

An Island (Traffic)

A roundabout. You may think that everyone calls them 'islands' but try using that when giving directions to a Southerner.

*

Argy–Bargy

An argument. An old English word deriving from the older Scottish, 'Argle–Bargle'.

*

Greebo

A 'greaser' or biker type. Probably from a shortening of the slang 'greaser', which in turn stemmed from the (usually correct) belief that motorcyclists were always covered in oil and grease - and those that rode

British bikes usually were.

*

Bobowler or Bob Howler

A big hairy moth. Probably Black Country, but an old Birmingham word in usage.

*

The Horse Road

Widely used in Birmingham to denote the road. Also Black Country 'oss road'. A language memory from pre motor vehicle days.

*

Pumps

Nothing to do with water. These go in a 'pump bag and hang on a peg at school. No Brummie would call them 'plimpsolls'.

*

Acky 1-2-3

A Birmingham variant of Hide and Seek, with

complex playground rules that require lawyers to unscramble. The 'Acky Post' was where the person 'on' would count up from. If the 'hiders' got back to the Post without being touched and shouted 'Acky 123' they were safe. I think......

*

Bostin

Brilliant, great, excellent. Claimed by both Black Country and Brummies and I'm not getting involved. What is beyond dispute is that it is our local Midlands word, not used elsewhere. It may derive from Anglo-Saxon 'bosten', meaning something to boast about. Be proud of it, and use it. (Also the name of our Facebook page and website *'Bostin Books',* please visit and 'like' us).

*

Our kid / Mom / Dad / Wench / The Nipper/ Nan / Gaffer

The family. 'Mom', not 'Mum' is the Brummie spelling. 'Our Kid' seems to be Brummie, but 'Our Wench' is Black Country. Brummies report being called 'the Nipper' from childhood through to their Seventies. Origin unknown. 'Nan' is Grandma of course, we didn't have enough 'ackers' for Nannies. 'Gaffer' is a very old word for grandfather but of course also 'boss'.

*

Yampy / Barmy / Barmpot

Mad, Crazy. Black Country. The 16th Century word, 'Barm', means frothing and excitable. 'Balmy' in the 1800's meant 'foolish'.

*

Tuppeny crush

This one dates back to the glory days of cinema. It was the queue for the cheap seats.

*

Jollop

Dad used this all the time, as in 'a drop of jollop'. It means medicine, usually cough medicine. The history is interesting. It most likely came from the English in India, where 'jalap' was grown as a commercial crop.

This was a drug made from a kind of Convulvulus that originated near the town of Jalapa, Mexico (as in Jalapeno peppers). British Army slang turned it into a general term for medicine.

*

A piece / A bad (h)and

A slice of bread (and butter), or a sandwich. As in, 'If you behave you'll get a jam piece' A 'bad (h)and' is somewhat obscure but seems to denote a jam 'doorstop'.

*

Caggy handed

Left handed. A midlands term because elsewhere people will tell you it is cack handed. And it isn't, so there.

*

The Outdoor

The Off–Licence or 'Offie'. A few Birmingham pubs actually had a signed 'Outdoor' attached to them.

*

A Cob

A bun, crusty or not. We could spend a lot of time on this – but we won't as we have lives to live.

*

Wallop

I remember two senses in which this was used. The first was beer. Out of interest, the term, 'codswallop' stems from derision towards 'Codd's non-alcoholic ginger beer'. The second was 'wallop the walls', which meant to paint (quickly).

*

Hard collar

Hard work. Origin quite murky, but it is suggested that this is gypsy slang. The connection of 'collar' to work seems to date back a long way and may refer to working horse collars, so perhaps dates from agricultural culture.

*

Snap

Food, can also mean a food break when working e.g. 'Snap–time'. Common Birmingham Police usage – 'book me in for snap'.

*

A Mop

Nothing to do with floors and of very old provenance. It is a Fair, but more accurately, a 'Trade and hiring' fair. Usually held in the Autumn following harvest when there was a slack period, those wishing to be hired would present themselves, armed with a token of their trade. Thus a shepherd would wear wool, and maids held small mops, from which the name sprang. There seems to have been a good deal of pleasure attached to the event in the form of drinking, feasting and general debauchery (pre-dating the 'Back Of Rackhams') And from memory, this aspect used to be celebrated effectively at the 'Kings Norton Mop' in more recent times!

*

Yam Yam

Our wonderful neighbours and intermarried ancestors from the Black Country. Do you know that the Black Country language is the closest modern dialect to that spoken by Chaucer – Middle English? Anyway, the term derives from the Black Country, 'you am'.

*

The Cut

The Canal - Black Country. I presume it stems from the canals being 'cut' out of the ground. 'Up the cut' means to go along the towpath, 'In the cut' is where the shopping trolleys go.

*

A Sarbut

A very local word that has ended up in Police slang, (see our book 'One In For D & D), where it means 'an informant'. There is some suggestion that it derives from the word 'saboteur', but there is evidence it dates back to at least the 1860's as 'Sarbot', denoting a gossip or tell-tale. Professor Chinn states it has a connection to men despatched by breweries incognito to check the correct brands were being served.

*

Cack-Handed

Clumsy, not dexterous with hands, can't wipe their
backside properly. Can also mean left–handed and is
linked to the Black Country 'cag-handed', which
means left – handed. The word 'cack' is 15th Century
Old English, meaning to void excrement, which in
turn comes from 'cacare', Latin for 'to defecate'.

*

Arf / Half– Soaked

Dozy, forgetful, slow-witted. A 'soak' is an old word
for a drunk.

*

Sterra & Fat

'Sterra' is Sterilised Milk, beloved of Bummies and
once delivered to the doorstep in reusable bottles
using electric vehicles. Pasteurised, 'Fat milk' came
in fat bottles in contrast to the tall, thin, 'Sterra' ones
and had different colour foil tops to denote the cream

content.

*

Monicker

A nickname. There is a suggestion this comes from
the Irish traveller language, the 'shelta' or 'cant', as
'munika'. Professor Carl Chinn states it comes from
tramp or Pedlar language and was used in
Birmingham to denote nicknames for illegal betting.
It is entirely plausible that the two are connected.

*

Fizzog

The face. The word is a slang version of
'physiognomy' - the facial features.

*

The Bog / Lar Pom

The toilet. It is alleged that 'Lar Pom' stems from the
Victorian habit of not referring directly to bodily
functions, so a posh-sounding word based on the
French 'La Pomme' – Apple was used. While we are
on this subject the 'Gazzunda' was the chamber pot

because it goes under the bed.

*

A dab (of) (hand)

'Dab hand' is an expert, a 'dab of' something is a light repeated touch. Neither are of Brummie origin, and both are potentially linked. It seems to date back at least as far as the early nineteenth century, and may be derived from Old Dutch 'dabben' and German 'tappen' If you want to be modern though, it is slang for a concentrated marijuana product and a 'hip – hop' dance. If you need to know what hip hop is, you are reading the right book, cos it ain't in here.

*

Cake-Hole

The mouth. Black Country. As in *'shut yer cake-hole'*

*

Gansey or Ganzey

A pullover. Comes from the word 'Guernsey' which is obvious when you think about it – it's close to

'Jersey'.

*

Pikelet

A type of crumpet. I kid you not, there are pages
about how it's cooked and how it differs from
crumpets and muffins and this book is too short for
that. The word apparently comes from Wales where a
'Bara -Pyglyd' is a type of spongy /'pitchy' bread.
Any road up, we used to have them toasted in front of
the gas fire then smothered in butter.

*

Palings

In Brum this generally means a fence, made of thin
upright panels or pales. The word dates back
hundreds of years and may link to 'palisade' which
was a protective fence around ancient settlements, so
dates back into antiquity.

*

Gully & Entry

A Gully in this context is a narrow street or

passageway. It comes from 'gullet' / gorge which indicates narrowing, as of the throat. Interestingly, in Hindi, 'Gully' means a street and I wonder whether the Days of The Raj have some connection with the term. An Entry is the alleyway between terraced houses.

*

Kaylied / Kaylie

This is a complicated one. Kaylie is a type of sherbert, not the powder type but crystalline, usually eaten by dipping a stick of liquorice into it. It may or may not have originated from a shortening of 'alkali' but no-one seems to know for sure.

'Kaylied' is a Midlands term for being drunk. It is no doubt a convoluted linkage between the slang word 'sherbert' meaning alcohol, usually beer, and Kaylie. The best pronunciation is Brummie where it sounds like 'Kayloy'.

*

Donnies

Hands – usually children's. 'Put ya gloves on yer

donnies'. 'Clean yer Donnies and you'll get a piece'.
Allegedly comes from the French 'Donez', 'to give'.
How it got into usage in Birmingham is anyone's
guess.

*

Dolally Tap

Someone who is mad. Originated in India in the late
nineteenth century. Deolali was a military transit
camp where troops often spent months waiting orders
whilst contracting various diseases and terminal
boredom in the heat or monsoon. 'Tapa' is Hindustani
for heat or fever, so the full slang phrase translates
more accurately as 'camp fever'.

*

Gormless

Stupid. An ancient word, 'gaum', meaning
'understanding', that in turn derives from The Norse
'gaumr' meaning 'care or heed'.

*

Reeky / Ronk /Riffy

Smelly or dirty. 'Reeky' derives from the Old English 'reac' – smoking, which had changed by the 1700s to mean smelling bad. Famously used by Shakespeare, *'the breath that from my mistress reeks'*, and he also used it to imply something that is suspicious or 'fishy'. 'Ronk' is a Northern word that probably combines 'rotten' and 'stink'. 'Riffy' seems to be Black Country.

*

Reasty

Food that's gone off. Dirty. Black Country.

*

Trankelments

Small possessions, ornaments or paraphernalia. Black Country. Also claimed by Yorkshire.

*

Gawping

To stare open–mouthed in wonder. Origin is the Old English word 'Gielpan', to boast, which is related to

———

14th Century 'galpen', to gape or yawn.

*

Rocks

Sweets. Often linked with the verb 'to crash', 'crash the rocks mate'. Can also be 'chobbled' vigorously.

*

Adams Ale

Pure water. All that Adam had to drink in the Garden of Eden. First written usage 1643, and became very popular within the Temperance movement in the 19th Century.

*

Fizzy Pop

As opposed to just 'pop', which is ordinary squash – without the bubbles. The fizzy stuff came via door-to-door delivery from the Alpine or Corona pop man, and I liked Dandelion and Burdock best.

*

A Benny

A slow or dull-witted person. A fairly modern piece of Brummie slang that relates to the character 'Benny', from the Midlands TV soap, 'Crossroads'.

*

Tip Tops and Jubbly's

Flavoured blocks of ice for kids, beloved of Brummies. A 'Tip Top' was a long thin one, the 'Jubbly' was a triangular / pyramidal shape. A good sucking usually extracted all the flavouring leaving a lump of ice that could often be put down the back of the unwary.

*

Jasper

A Wasp. Was in widespread British usage. It is thought to date back to at least medieval times and to be derived from the latin for a Wasp – 'vespa'.

*

Gamgee

Cotton wool. Joseph Gamgee was a surgeon at Birmingham General Hospital and in 1880 invented 'Gamgee Tissue', an absorbent cotton wool and gauze dressing. The name directly inspired J.R.R Tolkein to name Frodo Baggins' faithful companion, 'Sam Gamgee', in 'The Lord of The Rings'.

*

Jacksy

Not the Cockney one meaning backside. Ours means lucky, as in 'you jacksy bastard'.

*

Marlies / Glarneys

Either the game of marbles or the normal size marbles. The big ones were called 'Gobbies'. This seems to be a Midlands word.

*

Scrap

A fight. Probably derived from the old word 'scrape'.

*

Scraps and Bits

Leftover batter served with chips. Also called 'batterbits'.

*

Nunk

Nothing. No indication of origin.

*

Arly-Barley

A request for truce or surrender. May stem from French, 'Allez Parler' (Go and talk).

*

Barnacles

Spectacles. Dad used to call them this. No idea why.

*

Tatered

Tired. Can mean intoxicated but generally in Birmingham is used for fatigued, especially by the older population.

*

Mickey Mouse

A pint of Bitter and Lager mixed half and half.

*

Beezer

The iconic, Small Heath built, motorcycle. Slang for B.S.A which in turn stands for 'Birmingham Small Arms'. The company was begun in 1861 in the Gun Quarter in Birmingham and within two years bought land and built a factory at Armoury Road, Small Heath. Bicycle manufacture began in 1880, and motorcycles in 1910. A long and illustrious history followed, but all bikers of a certain age remember it for the motorcycles.

*

Brown and Mild

A pint of Mild Beer, (Ansells or M&B), coupled with a bottle of Mann's Stout.

*

Gnat's knacker

A unit of measurement used in Brummie engineering.

*

The Rezza

The Reservoir.

*

Bint

A girl. Comes from the identical Arabic word, meaning daughter or girl. Brought back to the UK after the British occupation of Egypt at the end of the 19th Century. Also *'bird'* as in *'Fred picked up a right nice bird at the Locarno'*

*

Bluenose

A long-suffering supporter of Birmingham City Football Club.

*

Garding

The Brummie garden.

*

Oroight

The classic Brummie greeting.

*

Ar

Yes

*

Bread an scrape

Not of Brummie origin and there is a difference of
opinion as to the reference. Some think it is bread
with thinly scraped butter, but I think it is bread and
meat dripping. Just writing it makes me want some.
Would make the Twitterati go pale, but dripping was
yummy and I realise now that I miss it lots....

*

Bang On

Spot on, exact.

*

The Garage

The Petrol Station.

*

Tig

The Brummie version of 'Tag', the children's game.

*

Dollop

A large shapeless mass – usually used in connection with food. A 16th Century English word that in turn comes from a Scandinavian word, probably 'dolp' which is Norwegian for 'lump'.

*

Cogwinder

A punch. A clout round the ear. Black Country.

*

Council Pop

Tapwater.

*

The Ostin

'The Austin', the legendary car company of Birmingham, manufacturer of such fine vehicles as the Austin Allegro. Later 'British Leyland', and now, unfortunately gone, the sad remnants owned by Shanghai Automotive.

*

Ackers

Money. Claimed as Cockney slang, but more likely brought back from Egypt by British troops as it is derived from the Arabic 'akka' which means a coin worth one piastre.

*

A note from the authors

If you enjoyed this book, please leave a review on its Amazon page. It will be much appreciated. If you want to know more about our Brummie / Midlands books, fiction and non – fiction, please visit our website **www.bostinbooks.co.uk** or our Facebook Page, 'Bostin Books'. I hope you enjoy them. 'Tara for now'.

Stephen Burrows (& Michael Layton).

February 2018